JUST IMAGINE!

7 Late Elementary Piano Solos That Encourage Expressive, Imaginative Playing

MARTHA MIER

Contents

Foreword

A piano student will perform music with more expression and feeling when he or she is able to see or imagine a mental image of what the music is about.

Just Imagine!, Book 2 contains seven solos in which the student can easily picture the image portrayed in the music. The gentle sounds of "The Black Swan" paint a picture of a graceful black swan gliding serenely across a beautiful and peaceful lake. Feel the excitement of "Hamster Chase" with its fast and spirited tempo, or imagine the humorous antics of a monkey scampering about a carousel in "Monkey on a Carousel."

Fly on the wings of your imagination, and enjoy the variety of moods, colors and styles found in *Just Imagine!*

Martha Mier

Artwork: Liana Kelley
Cover Design: Lisa Barrett
Music Engraving: Nancy Butler

Hamster Chase

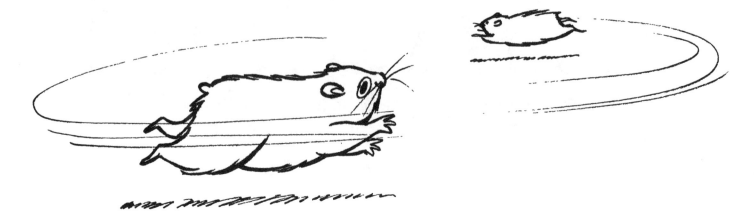

Martha Mier

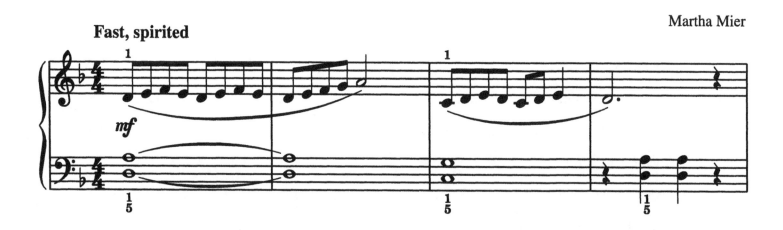

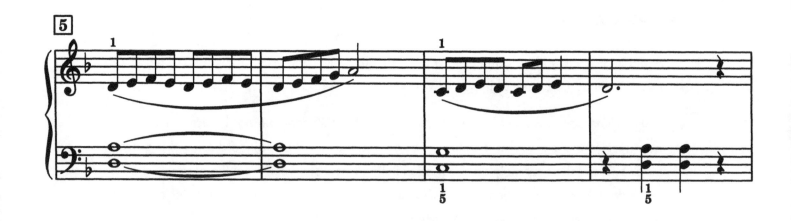

3

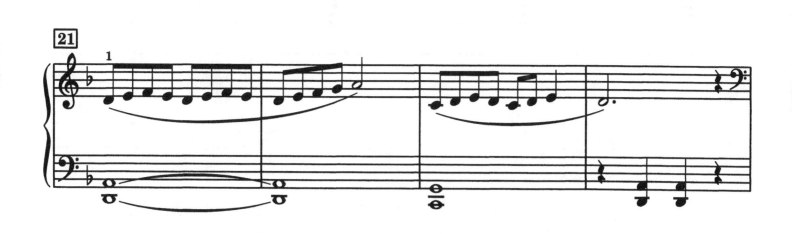

4

for Cortney Taylor

The Black Swan

Martha Mier

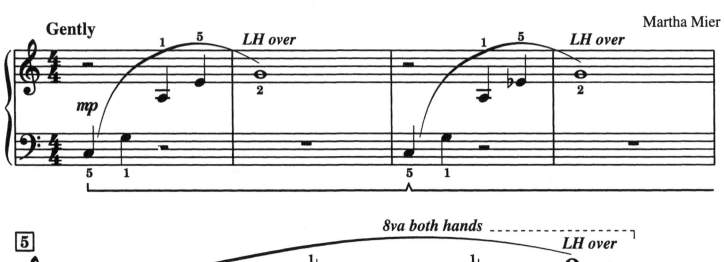

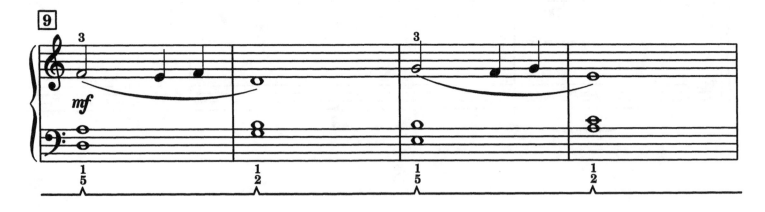

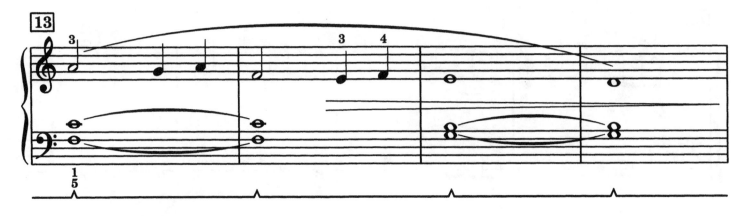

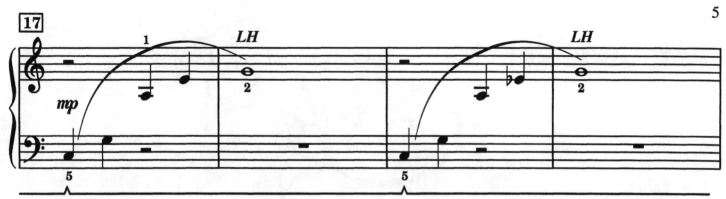

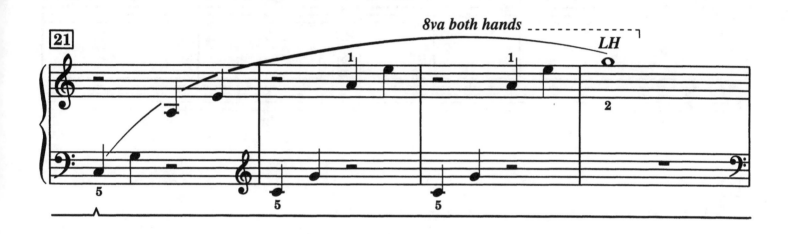

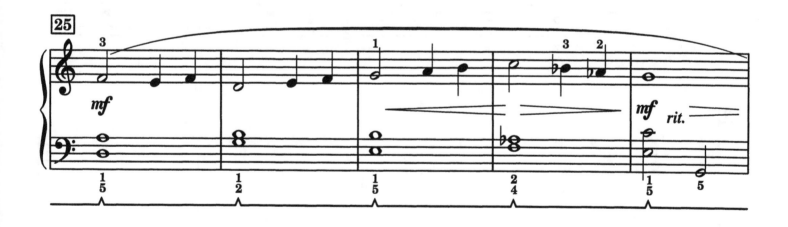

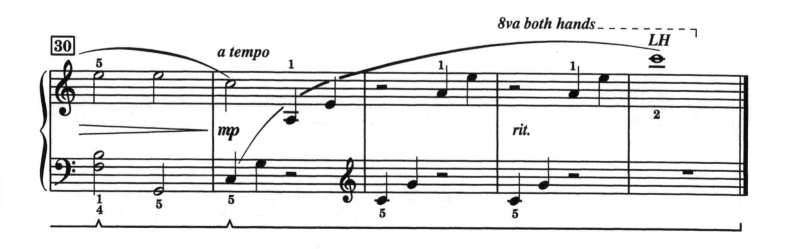

At a Dude Ranch

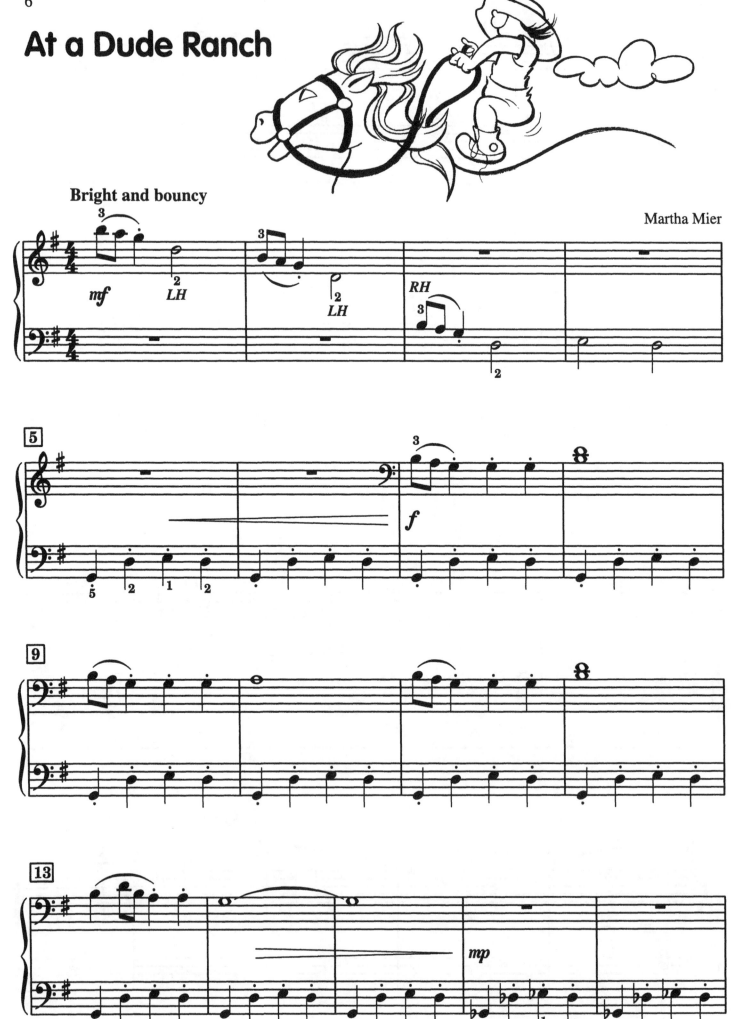

Martha Mier

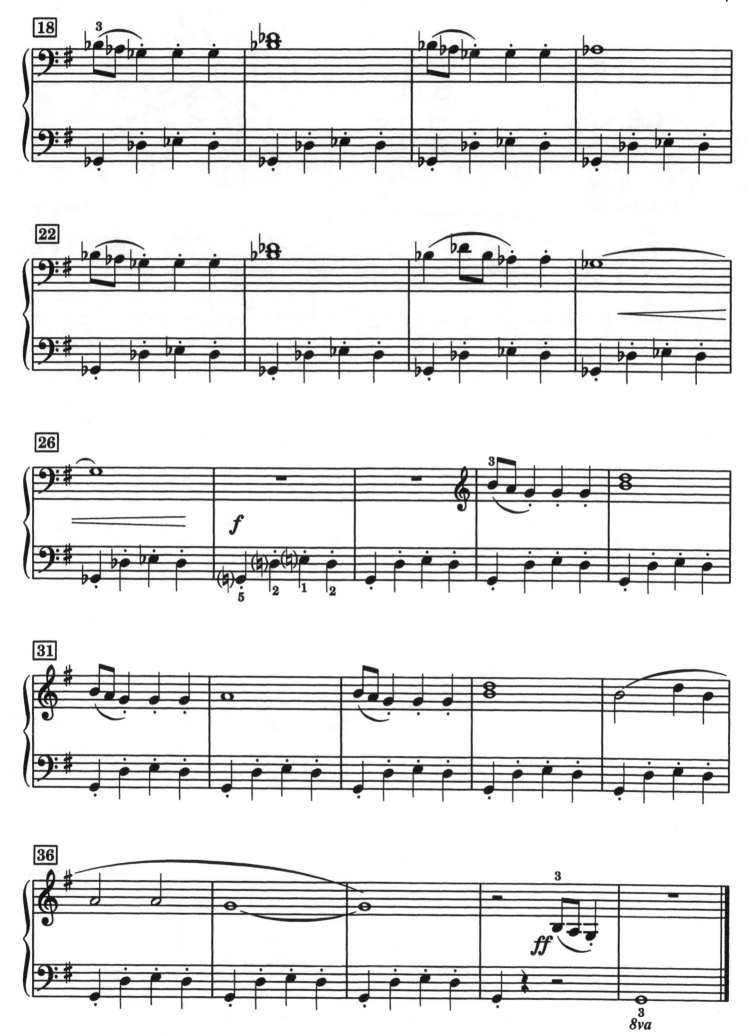

for Amy Herschleb

English Rose Gardens

With simplicity

Martha Mier

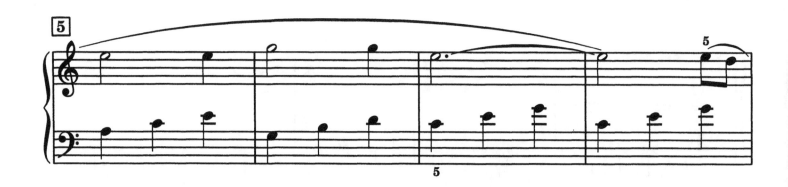

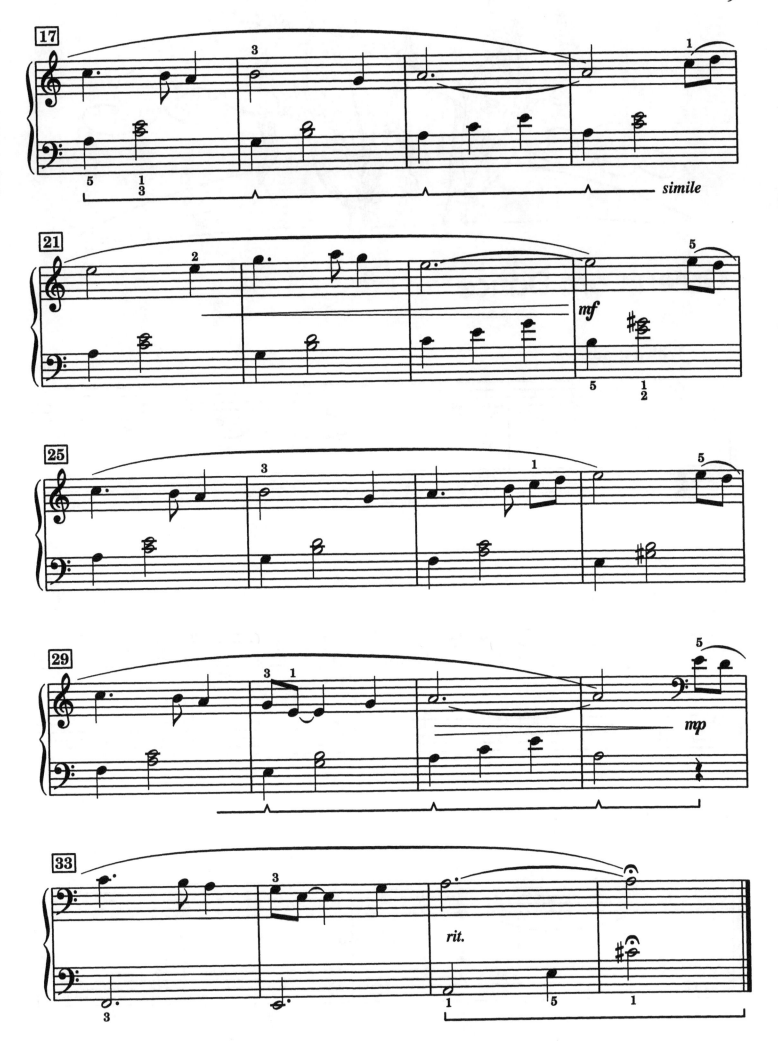

Green Corn Dance

With a steady beat

Martha Mier

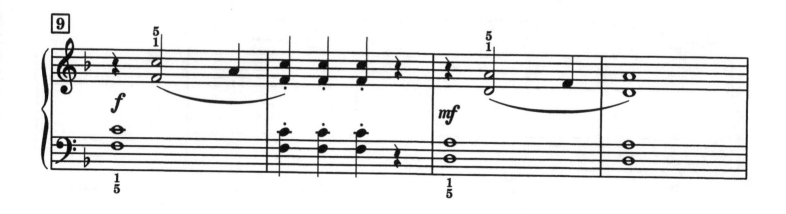

Little White Church

Martha Mier

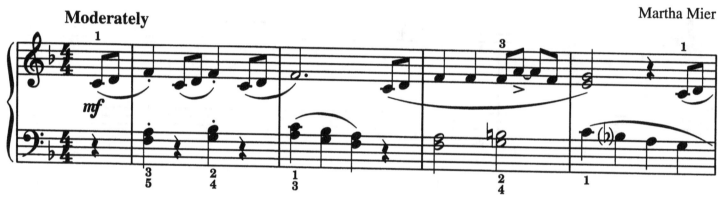

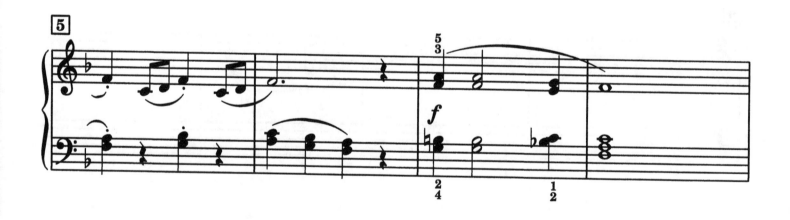

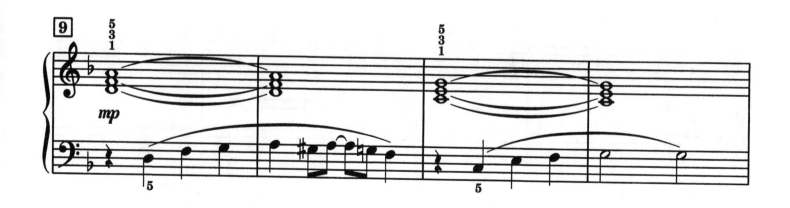

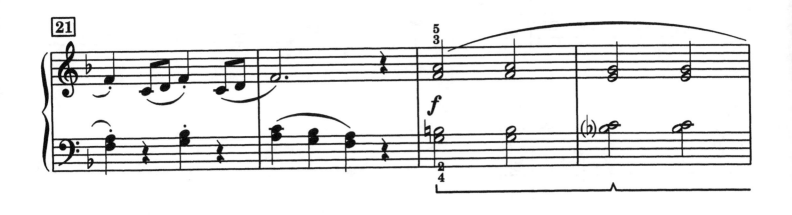

Monkey on a Carousel

Martha Mier

Cheerfully